THOUGHTS & PRAYERS

1LIKE
=
1PRAYER

You're an asshole. Go fuck yourself

1 hour ago · Like · 👍 2 Reply

Josh Latta, really??? Aside from the horrific implications of your statement, you're denying God's power in committing such an act. We don't always know why things are happening they way they are, but killing our children is never the answer.

7 minutes ago   Like

Mr. Josh Latta i will pray for you. And kirk Cameron you are a great person and a true inspiration

2 minutes ago · Like

Josh, I'm gonna pray every night for you that the Holy Spirit will show up and speak the truth to you. Jesus loves you so much and he wants a relationship with you!

4 minutes ago · Like

THAT'S A **HORRIBLE** THING TO SAY, JOSH LATTA!

UNDERWORLD AMUSEMENTS

isbn: 978-1-9436870-0-8

Edited and designed by Kevin I. Slaughter
for Underworld Amusements, LLC.
www.UnderworldAmusements.com

say that to a real new yorkers face,

2 hours ago · Like

Josh, if you actually looked at the Bible, you would see that God created sex to be between a husband and wife. The only time sex it wrong is when it is outside those confines.

4 minutes ago · Like

Go fuck yourself you piece of shit.

27 minutes ago · Like

You're a bitch. I know you. You're a fuck boy bitch. Mock 9/11?

And you lost business cause I've been trying to get my job to purchase about 20 custom drawings from you.

Like Reply

That's a horrible thing to say Josh Latta!

a few seconds ago via mobile · Like

Thoughts & Prayers

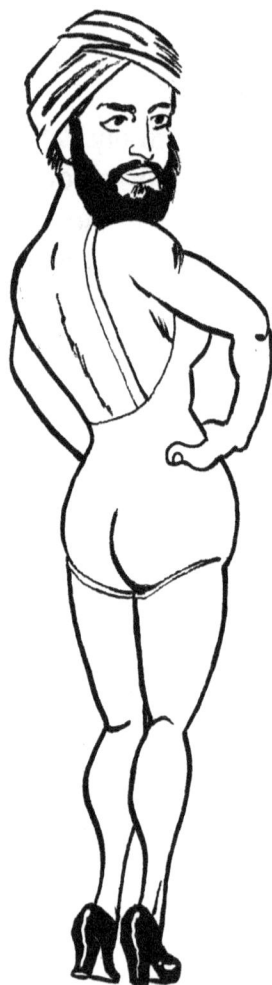

Wear this dress, be grateful to Allah and
walk like a bride dragging her skirts.

6

PART I
THE BRIMSTONES

OF COURSE I TREAT YOU LIKE A PIECE OF MEAT.
A PIECE OF MEAT THAT I LOVE.

Tasty Brimstones

I CAN'T STAND TO SEE YOU HAPPY.

We R The Brimstones

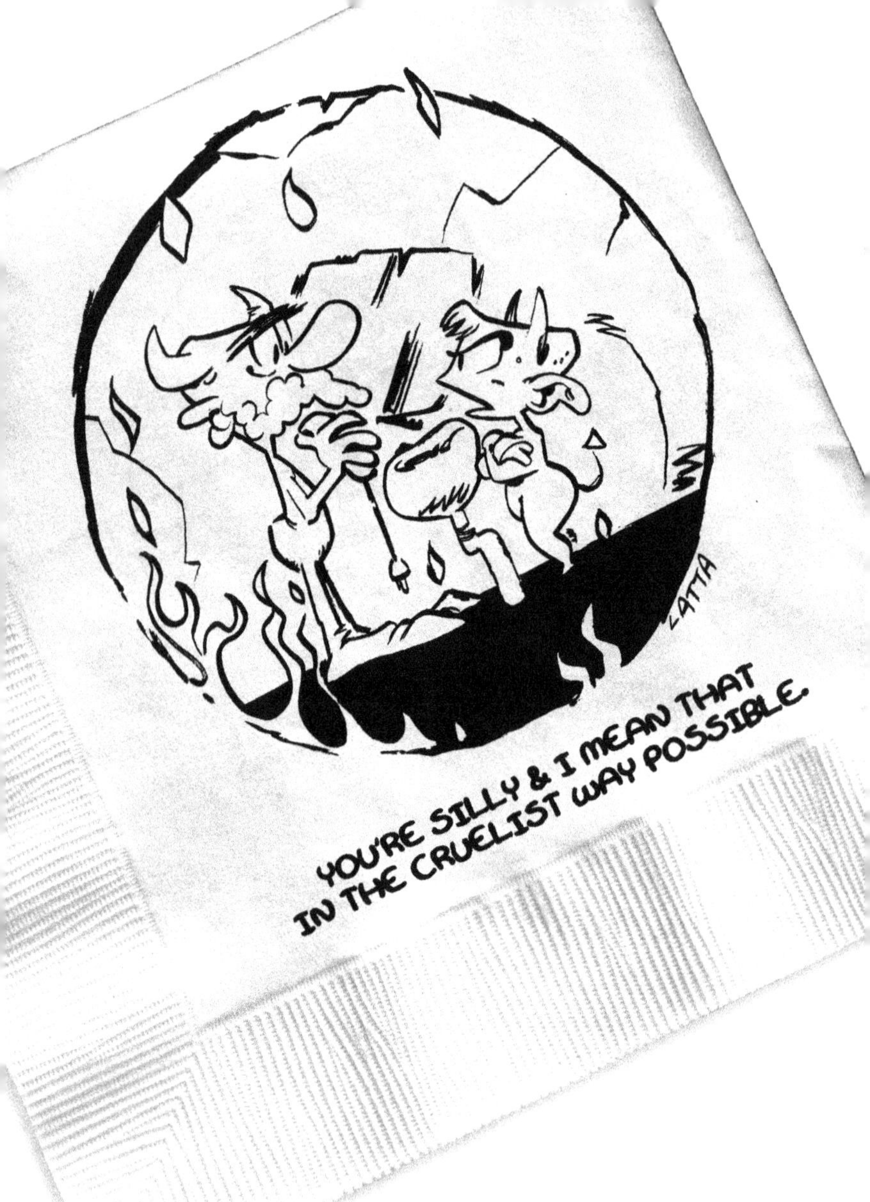
LATTA
YOU'RE SILLY & I MEAN THAT IN THE CRUELIST WAY POSSIBLE.

Brimstones R Back

Brimstones Roasting On An Open Fire

THE ONLY REASON I WENT BOWLING WITH YOU IS TO LAUGH AT YOUR SHORTCOMINGS.

Keepin' Score With The Brimstones

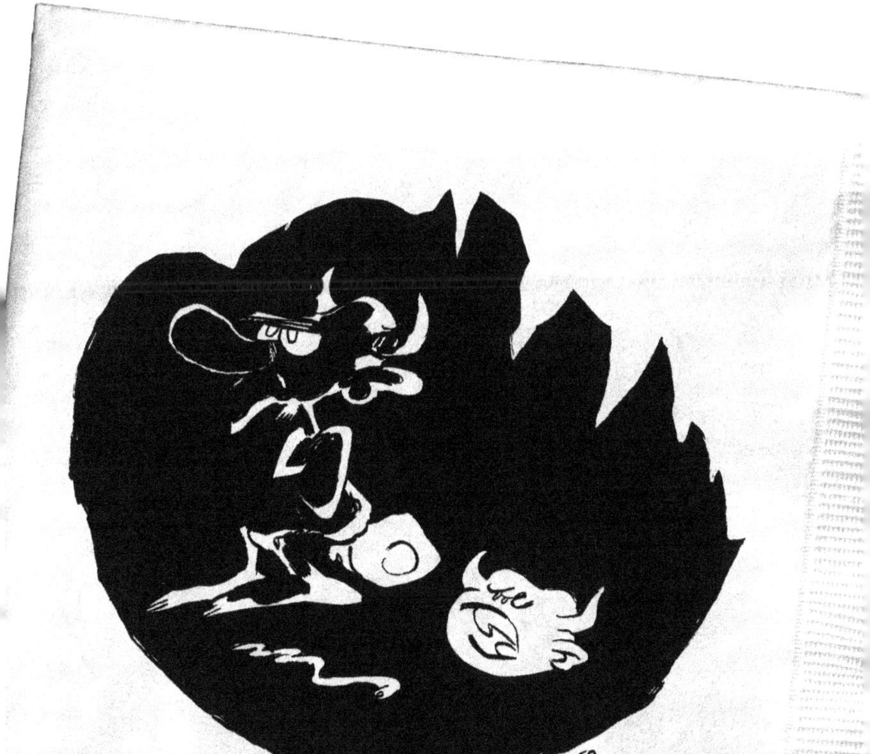
LATTA
YOU CAN'T STAND IT WHEN I LOOK PRETTY, CAN YOU?

Mean Ol' Brimstones

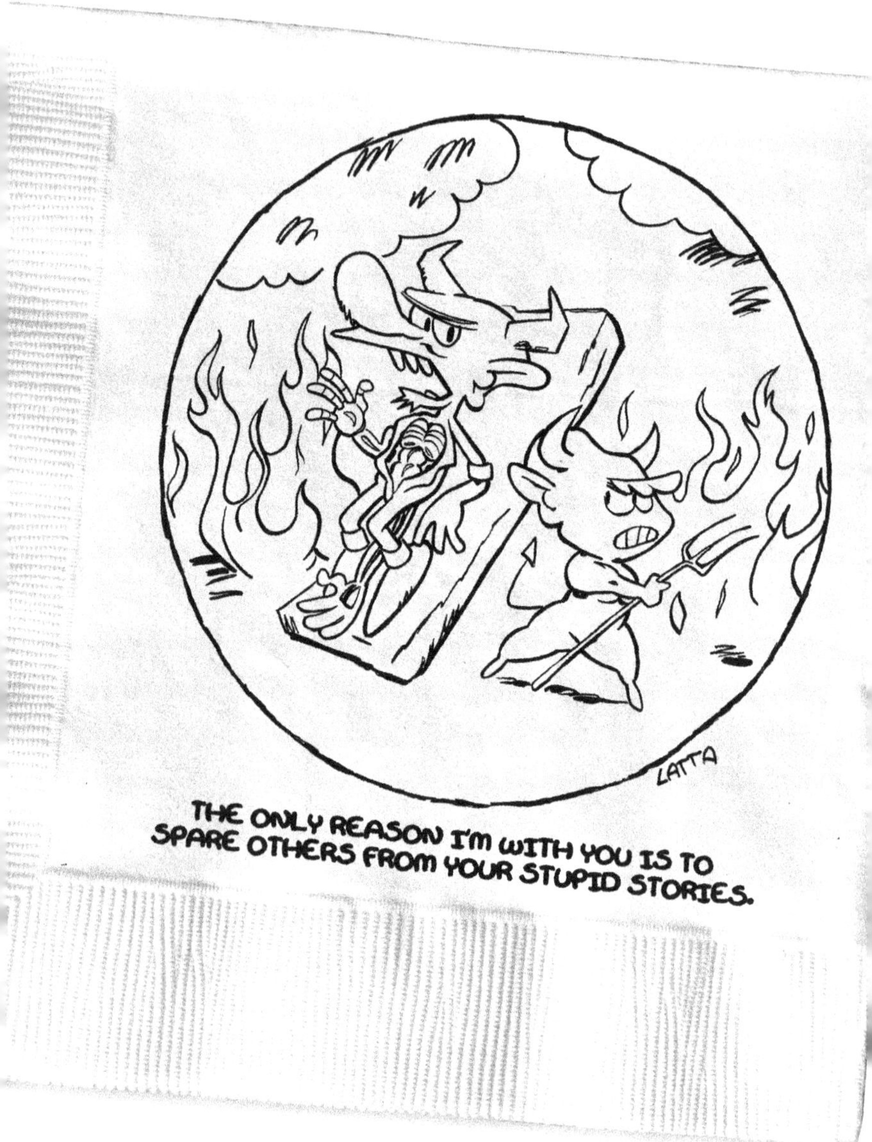
LATTA
THE ONLY REASON I'M WITH YOU IS TO SPARE OTHERS FROM YOUR STUPID STORIES.

Oh No, It's The Brimstones

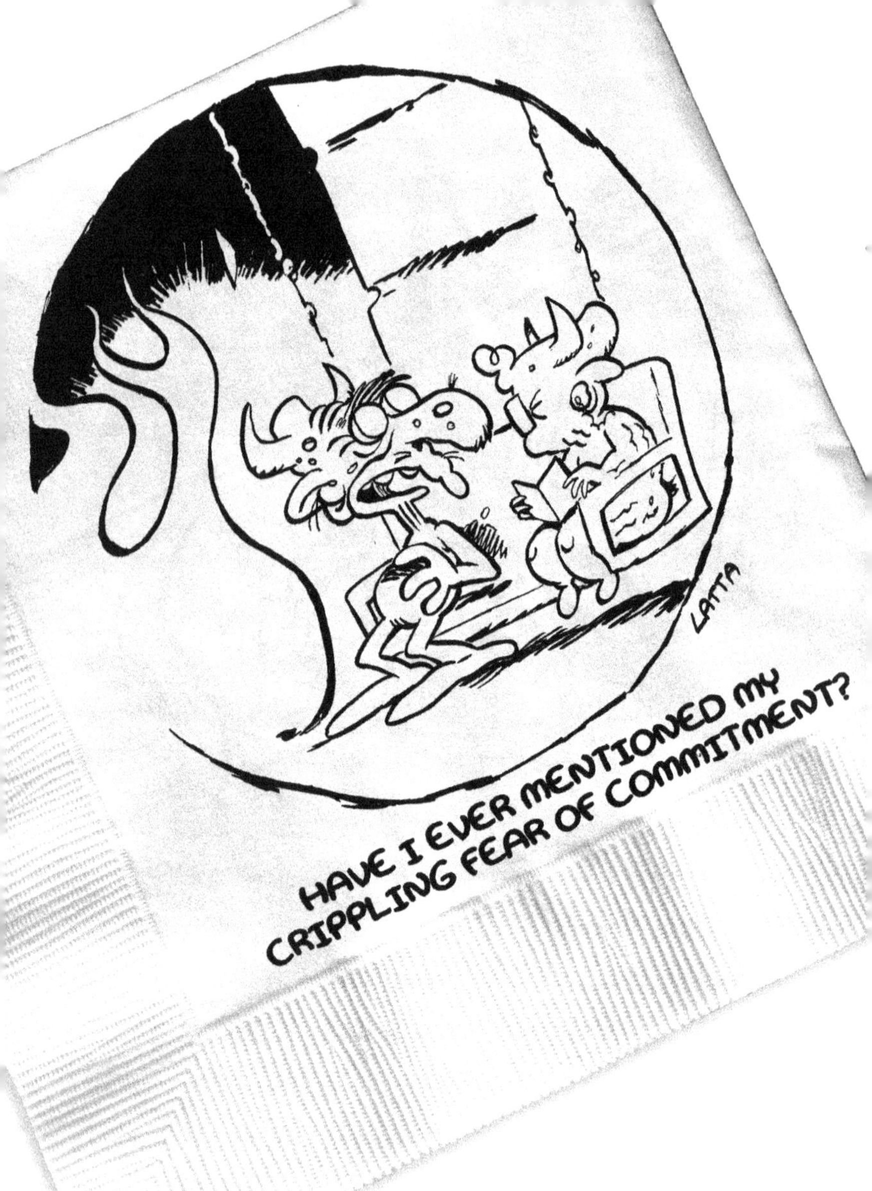
LATTA
HAVE I EVER MENTIONED MY
CRIPPLING FEAR OF COMMITMENT?

We R The Brimstones.

I'M NEVER SURE WHAT TO DO WITH MY HANDS AT THESE ORGIES.

Brimstones 2099

17

It's That Time of the Month, Brimstones.

Work Stinks, Brimstones

Brimstones in "Just Married"

20

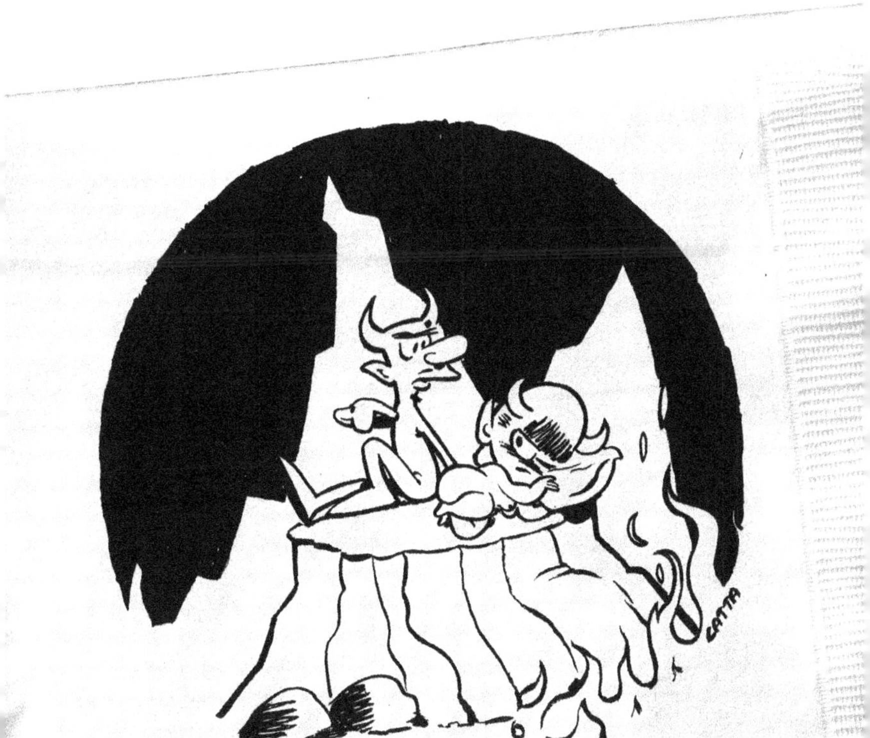
WHAT ABOUT MY NEEDS & MY DESIRES?
LIKE MY DESIRE TO BE CRUEL TO YOU.

The Brimstones

YOU'RE STILL HERE?

Meet The Brimstones

PART II
FUN FACTS!

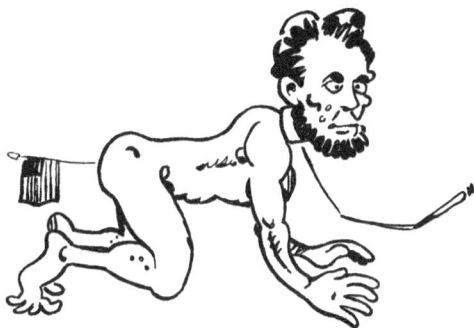

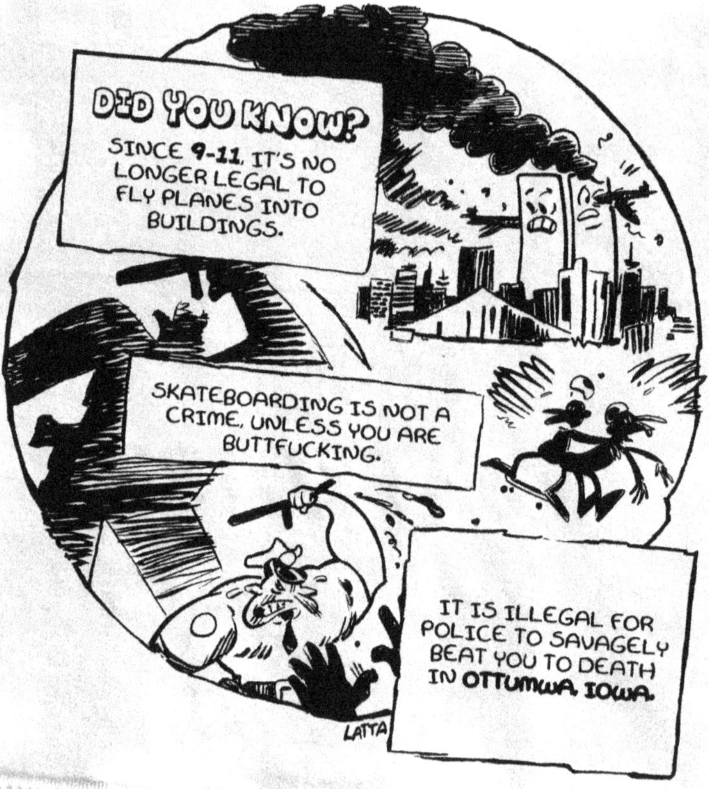
DID YOU KNOW?
SINCE 9-11, IT'S NO LONGER LEGAL TO FLY PLANES INTO BUILDINGS.
SKATEBOARDING IS NOT A CRIME, UNLESS YOU ARE BUTTFUCKING.
IT IS ILLEGAL FOR POLICE TO SAVAGELY BEAT YOU TO DEATH IN OTTUMWA, IOWA.
LATTA

FUN FACT:

VAN HALEN'S NUMBER ONE SMASH HIT, "RUNNING WITH THE DEVIL" WAS ORIGINALLY CALLED "TAKING A SHIT WITH THE DEVIL."

FUN FACT:

IT'S A COMMON MISCONCEPTION THAT THE TOILET WAS INVENTED BY THOMAS CRAPPER. IT WAS ACTUALLY CREATED BY JONATHAN TAKEASHIT.

LATTA

FUN FACT:
PEARL HARBOR ACTUALLY HOUSED MORE THAN THIRTEEN THOUSAND DILDOS WHEN IT EXPLODED.
...STUDIES HAVE SHOWN THAT WALK-IN COOLERS ARE AN EXCELLENT PLACE TO GET HIGH.
BANG!
FUN FACT:
SUICIDE IS ALWAYS AN OPTION.
LATTA

DID YOU KNOW?
THE FIRST DRAFT OF THE CONSTITUTION CONTAINS THE WORD "FUCK" THREE TIMES.
86% OF AMERICAN FAMILIES ARE MENTALLY RETARDED.
...I AM BUT A BRAIN IN A JAR.
LATIA

FUN FACTS:
THE EARTH SHALL
ROT/YOUR CHILDREN
WILL BE DEFORMED.

FUN FACT!
YOU'LL NEVER
FINISH THAT
BOOK.

DID YOU KNOW?
ABE LINCOLN WAS CREATED
BY HALLMARK TO COMBAT
LAGGING PRESIDENTS DAY
CARD SALES.

LATTA

FUN FACTS:
IF YOU TOOK ALL THE BAGEL BITES® IN THE WORLD AND STACKED THEM UP, ONE ON TOP OF ANOTHER, IT'D BE PRETTY COOL.

...IF YOU WERE IN A COMA, YOUR PETS WOULD MISS YOU LESS AND LESS EACH DAY UNTIL YOU ARE COMPLETELY FORGOTTEN.

LATTA

FUN FACT: STAN LEE ALMOST NAMED HIS FAMOUS COMIC MAGAZINE, "FANTASTIC FIVE" UNTIL HE REALIZED THERE WERE ONLY FOUR OF THEM.

FUN FACT: THE CREATOR OF KRAZY KAT, GEORGE HERRIMAN, ALWAYS WORE A HAT TO HIDE THE FACT THAT HE WAS MISSING THE TOP OF HIS SKULL.

LATTA

PART III

SUICIDE NOTES

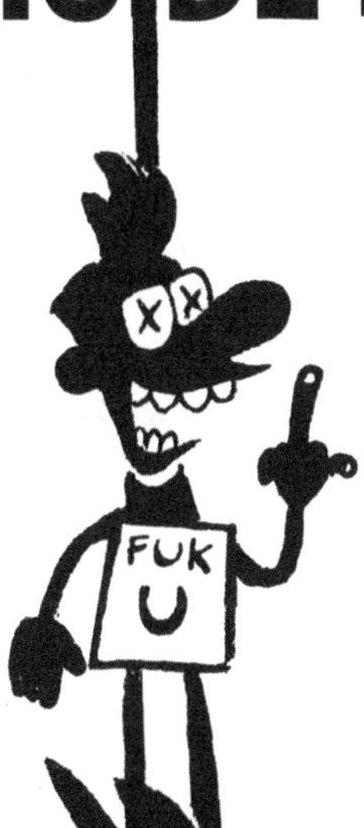
FUK
U

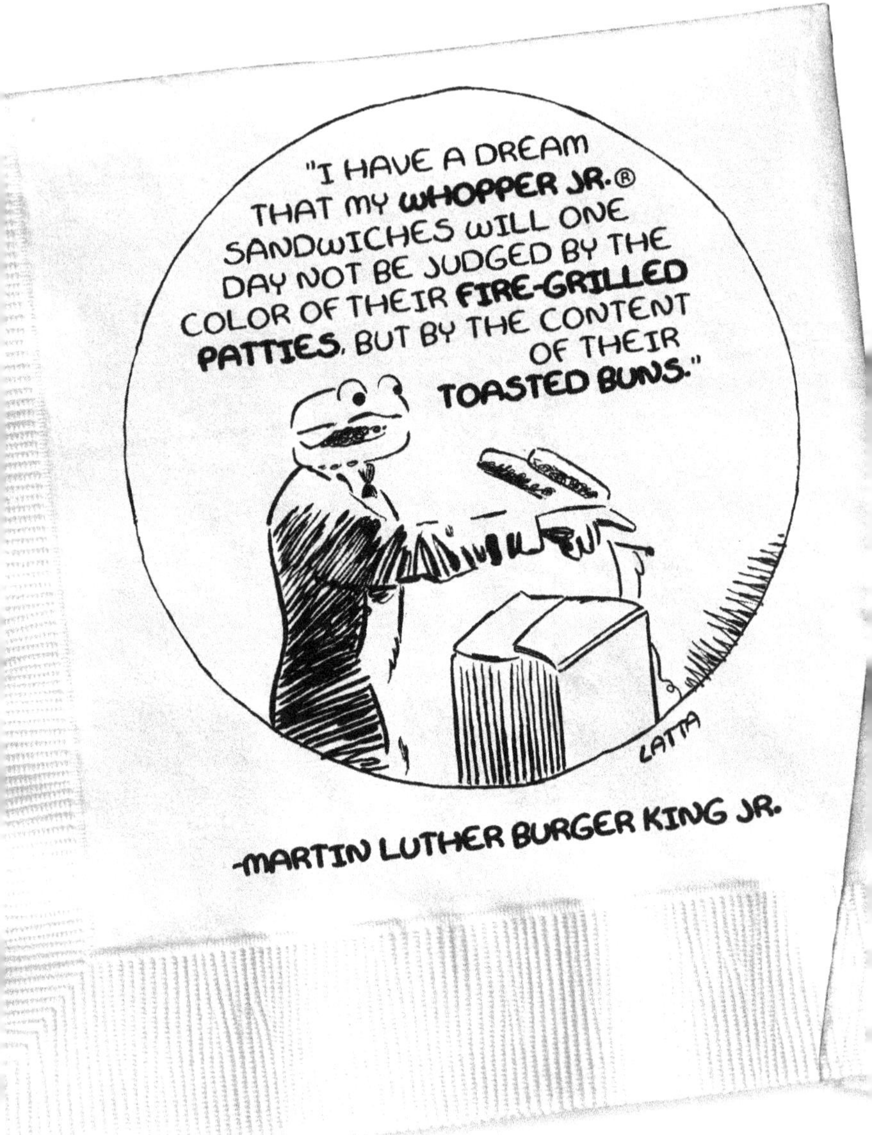
"I HAVE A DREAM THAT MY WHOPPER JR.® SANDWICHES WILL ONE DAY NOT BE JUDGED BY THE COLOR OF THEIR FIRE-GRILLED PATTIES, BUT BY THE CONTENT OF THEIR TOASTED BUNS."
LATTA
-MARTIN LUTHER BURGER KING JR.

...THE BAD NEWS? FOUR OF YOUR VIRGINS WERE CARTOONISTS.

Holy Crap

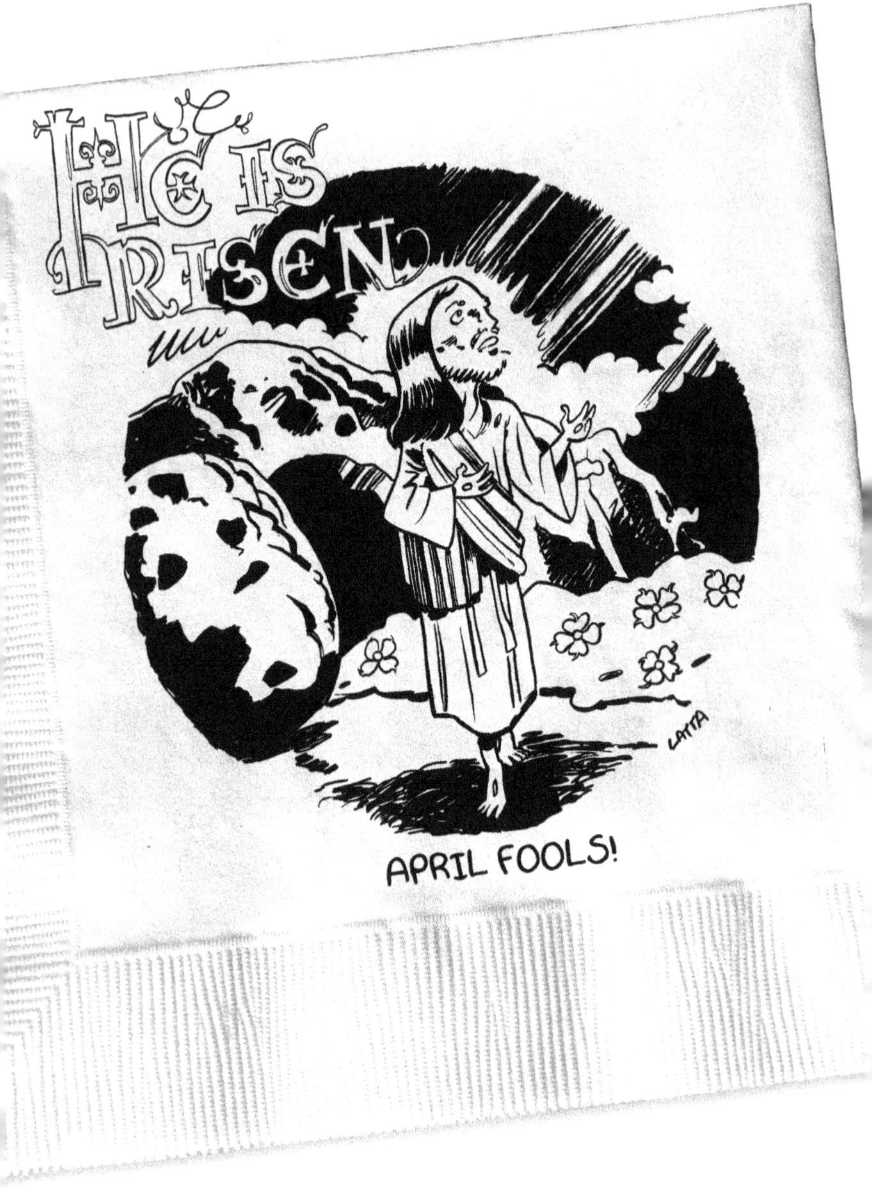
HE IS RISEN
LATTA
APRIL FOOLS!

Easter Funday

"I HAVE NO REGRETS, FOR YOU SEE, THE CIVIL WAR HAS BEEN VERY FUN."

Most Likely to Secede

I REALLY DO HOPE THIS IS THE APOCALYPSE. MY PHONE PLAN IS OUT OF DATA.

It's the End of the World
as We Know It, and I Feel Furious.

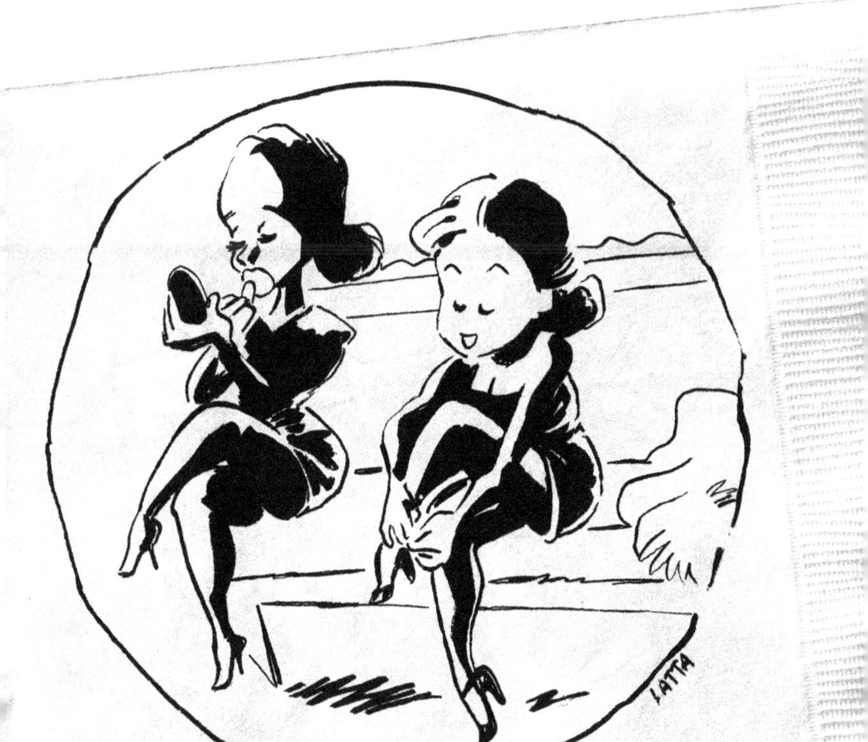
LATTA
IDEAS ARE LIKE ASSHOLES.
WE LIKE TO DATE THEM.

UHH, THIS IS A BIT AWKWARD, BUT DID YOU RECEIVE MY DEATH THREATS?

Keeping Up With the Jones

WE HAVE ALL THE SAME INTERESTS. —LIKE OUR NEXT FIX.

Baltimore Funnies

ALL MY LIFE I'VE BEEN CHASING THE COOL SIDE OF THE PILLOW.

It's 4am Somewhere

I HAD THIS CRAZY DREAM THAT I HAD TO USE MY GRANDMOTHER'S FOOT AS A BONG.

Stems and Shake

Hear My Voice, Hear My Butt

I'VE SEEN YOUR BUTTHOLE ON THE INTERNET.

Poopdeck (On the)

4 3

Comics Aren't for Kids Anymore

Choose Your Own Punchline

I LOVE CUTE HATS, BUT I HAVE MORE OF A PLUNGER-ON-MY-HEAD FACE.

Women R the Same Everywhere

TIME TO JACK OFF!

Julio Iglesias

47

I COULD TAKE ALL YOUR PROBLEMS AND GIVE THEM TO SOMEONE LESS PRETTY.

Erin & Josh

EVEN WITH CLOTHES ON, YOU ARE STILL A NAKED CHICK TO ME.

Josh & Erin

ACTUALLY, THIS ISN'T AS BAD
AS I THOUGHT IT'D BE.

Erin & Josh in Grim and Bare It.

OH, HAVEN'T YOU HEARD? I'M INTO OLD-TIMEY FINGERING NOW.

My Word!

WHAT, YOU THINK I CREATED YOU FOR INTELLIGENT CONVERSATION?

Halloween Laffs

ARE BANKS EVEN OPEN TODAY?

Halloween Funnies

I STILL CAN'T BELIEVE STEVE CARELL DIED IN THAT MANNER.

Comic From the Future

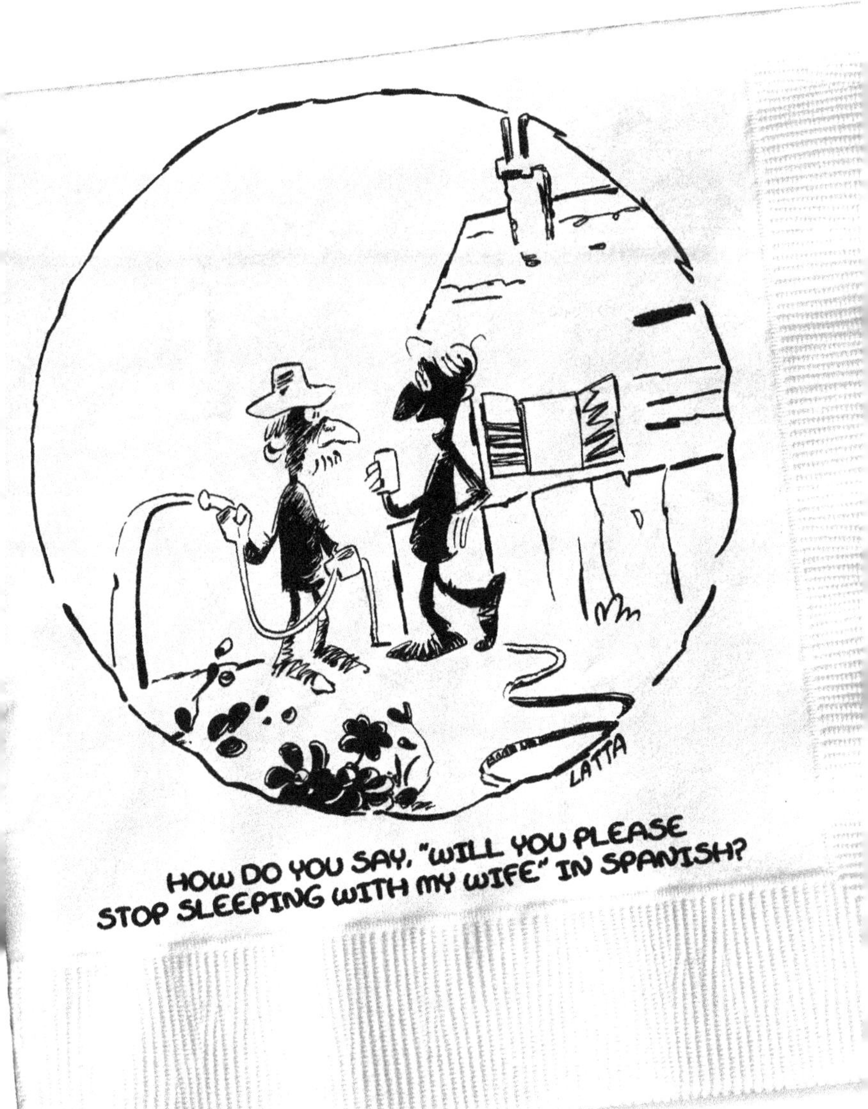
LATTA
HOW DO YOU SAY, "WILL YOU PLEASE
STOP SLEEPING WITH MY WIFE" IN SPANISH?

Juan in a Million

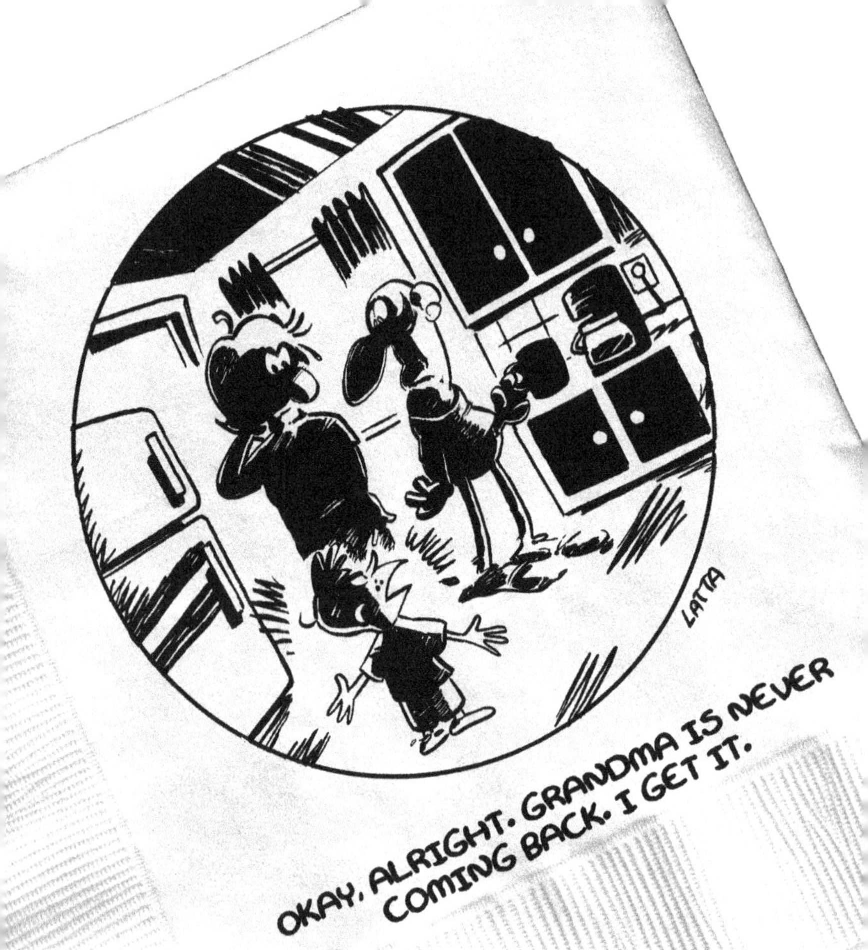
LATTA
OKAY, ALRIGHT. GRANDMA IS NEVER COMING BACK. I GET IT.

LOOKS TO ME LIKE YOU GOT TOO-TIGHT PUSSYITUS.

Spreader of Old Wive's Tails

DO YOU THINK WE CAN STILL BE FRIENDS?

Right Now I'm Not Ready for This Kind of Relationship.

...A PUPPY TO SHARE CHOCOLATE WITH.

Happiness Is...

59

I AM THE ANGEL OF DEATH. I AM DEATH. I'M JUST KIDDING.

AT LEAST YOUR MANI-PEDIS WILL BE HALF PRICE.

Boy George Was Right. War IS Stupid.

"GAY."

Boy George Was Right. War IS Stupid.

PERSONALLY, I DON'T TRUST ANYONE MADE OF LAMPSHADES.

Boy George Was Right. War IS Stupid.

"NEAT!"

Husbands Like Me

64

SHIA LABEOUF NEEDS TO STOP PLAYIN.

What's In the News Today

AFTER ALL THESE YEARS I STILL CAN'T BELIEVE WE HAD ANAL SEX BEFORE WE HAD REGULAR SEX.

Old Folks

66

CAN'T A GUY PISS IN HIS YARD AT CHRISTMASTIME?

May All Your Christmases Be Yellow

THIS PLACE SMELLS LIKE PUSSY.

Desert Isle Comics

68

I HATE RAP MUSIC.

Kantankerous Komix

69

RIP: RICHARD DREYFUSS

"We are gonna need a bigger boat."

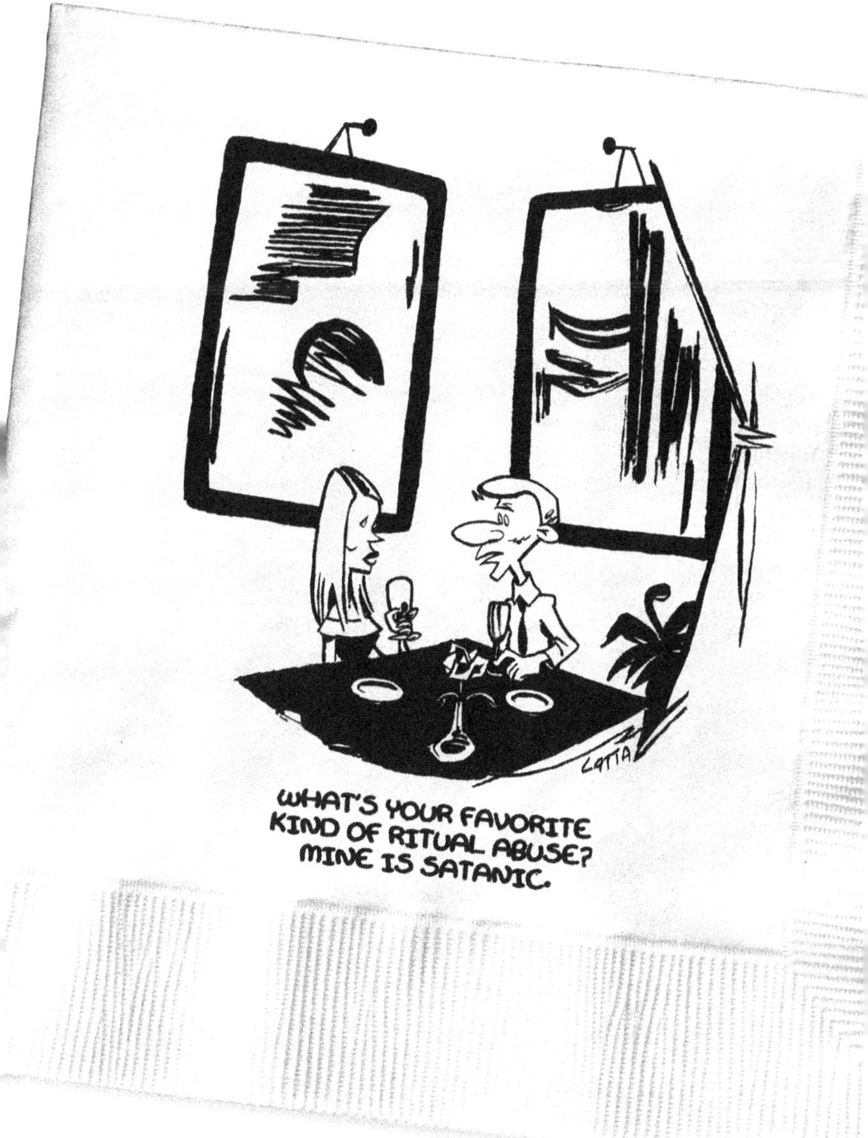
LOTTA
WHAT'S YOUR FAVORITE
KIND OF RITUAL ABUSE?
MINE IS SATANIC.

Ritual Abuse Date

I'M PRETTY DISAPPOINTED I WASN'T MENTIONED IN YOUR SUICIDE NOTE.

Suicide Funnies

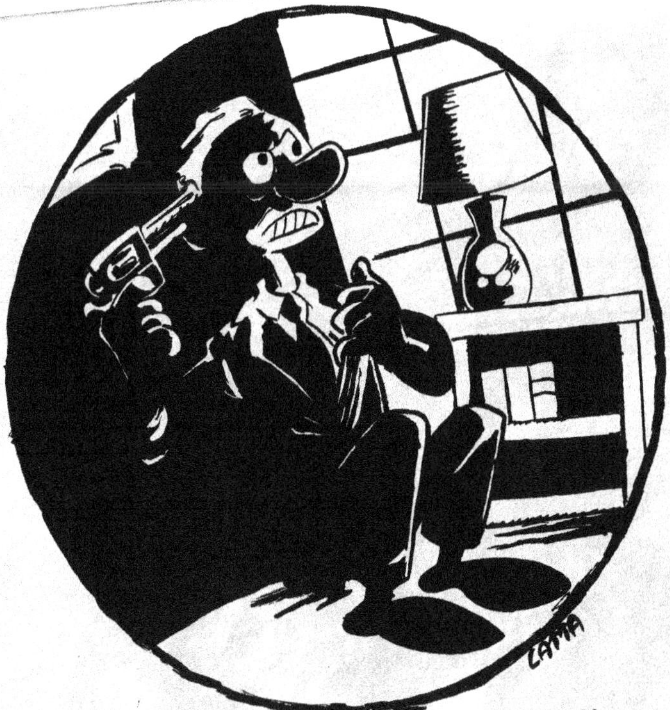
LAMA

I LAID WASTE TO A BUTTERFLY.
I JUST WANTED TO TEACH IT A LESSON
ABOUT BEING BEAUTIFUL.

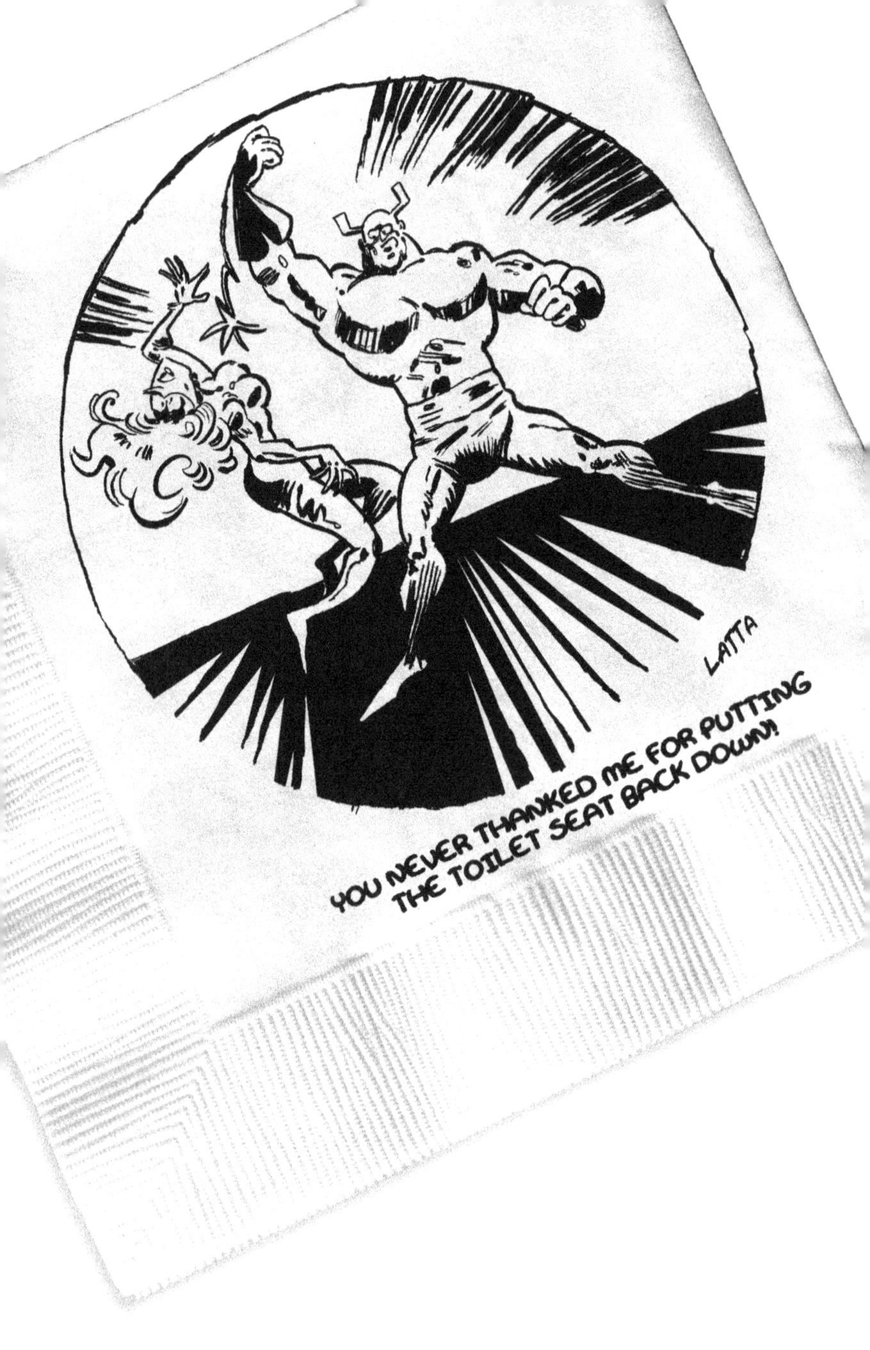
LATTA
YOU NEVER THANKED ME FOR PUTTING
THE TOILET SEAT BACK DOWN!

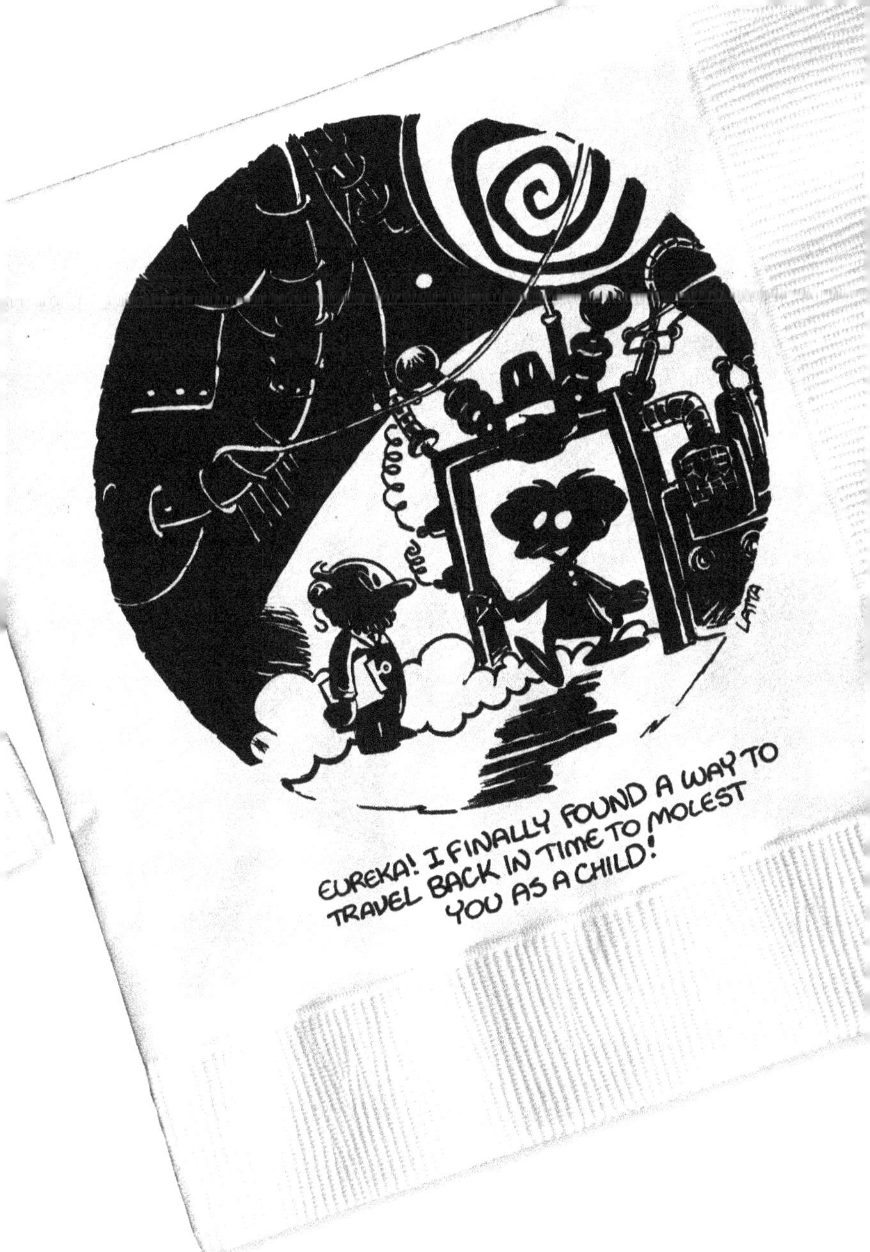
LATTA
EUREKA! I FINALLY FOUND A WAY TO
TRAVEL BACK IN TIME TO MOLEST
YOU AS A CHILD!

Gotta Get Back

THERE ARE TWO KINDS OF PEOPLE IN THIS WORLD. THOSE WHO PISS THE SHIT OFF THE SIDE OF THE TOILET, AND THOSE WHO DON'T.

These Two Men Are In Fact Quite Lucky to Have Gotten This Non-profit Position Through the Outreach Program at the New School for Social Research.

SO, THIS IS MY LIFE.

Mondays...

ALL BABIES ARE WORKS OF ART.
WORKS OF ART YOU MAKE WITH YOUR PUSSY.

LATTA

Moms Like Us.

www.ingramcontent.com/pod-product-compliance
Lightning Source LLC
Chambersburg PA
CBHW020516030426
42337CB00011B/420

9781943687008